TULSA CITY-COUNTY LIBRARY

owjc
11/11

D1116318

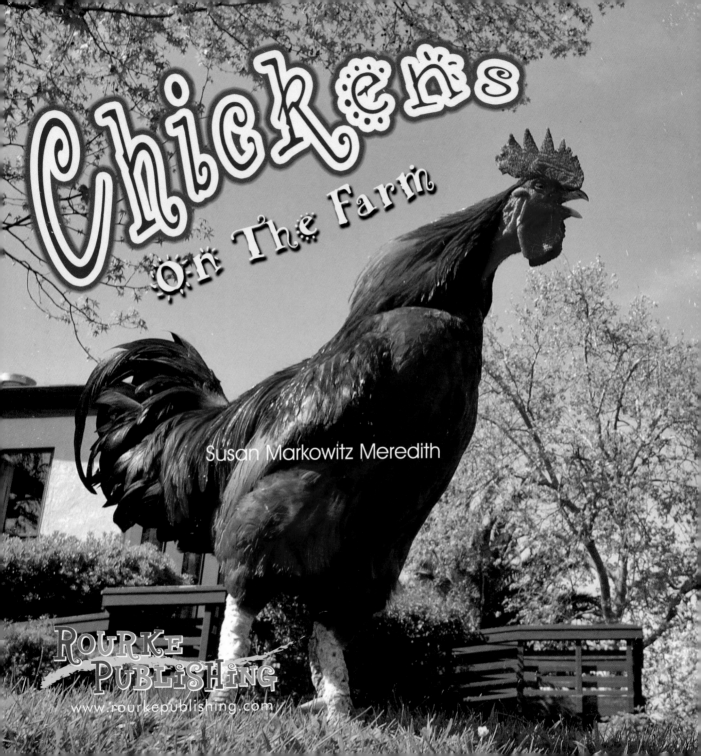

Chickens
on The Farm

Susan Markowitz Meredith

ROURKE
PUBLISHING
www.rourkepublishing.com

© 2011 Rourke Publishing LLC

All rights reserved. No part of this book may be reproduced or utilized in any form or by any means, electronic or mechanical including photocopying, recording, or by any information storage and retrieval system without permission in writing from the publisher.

www.rourkepublishing.com

PHOTO CREDITS: Title Page: © Mark Rasmussen; Page 3: © Burack Demir; Page 5: © Sandeep Subba; Page 7: © pongpol boonyen; Page 9: © Marilyn Barbone, © Jerry Moorman, © Eli Franssens, © Ladd Van Tol; Page 11: © Roberto A Sanchez; Page 12: © Barbara Tripp; Page 13: © Duncan Noakes; Page 15: © PhotoTalk; Page 17: © underumbrella; Page 19: © David Claassen; Page 20: © Gina Hanf, © joingate, © Luis Carlos Torres; Page 21: © malerpaso; Page 2: © jarenwicklund Background: © Douglas Philipon

Edited by Precious McKenzie

Cover by Nicola Stratford, Blue Door Publishing
Interior design by Tara Raymo

Library of Congress Cataloging-in-Publication Data

Meredith, Susan, 1951-
Chickens on the farm / Susan Markowitz Meredith.
    p. cm. -- (On the farm)
Includes bibliographical references and index.
ISBN 978-1-61590-264-4 (Hard Cover) (alk. paper)
ISBN 978-1-61590-504-1 (Soft Cover)
1. Chickens--Juvenile literature. 2. Farm life--Juvenile literature. I. Title.
SF487.5.M474 2011
636.5--dc22

                    2010009850

Rourke Publishing
Printed in the United States of America, North Mankato, Minnesota
033010
033010LP

www.rourkepublishing.com - rourke@rourkepublishing.com
Post Office Box 643328 Vero Beach, Florida 32964

Table of Contents

Chickens Here and There

Chickens are farm birds. All over the world farmers raise chickens for their eggs and meat. Today, more than 16 billion chickens live on Earth.

FUN FACT

Poultry *is another name for farm birds that people raise for meat and eggs. Chickens, ducks, geese, and turkeys are types of poultry.*

5

Thousands of years ago, chickens were wild. At first, people hunted these wild birds. Over time, they began to feed the wild birds and keep them close by for their eggs and meat.

All chickens once looked like red jungle fowl. These wild birds come from Southeast Asia.

Today, there are many kinds, or **breeds**, of chickens. Each breed has a special **quality**, such as the size or color of its eggs, the taste of its meat, or even the look of its feathers.

FUN FACT

Adult male chickens, or roosters, are usually larger and more colorful than adult females, called hens.

Common Chicken Breeds:

Leghorn lays more white eggs than any other breed.

Plymouth Rock produces good-tasting meat.

Rhode Island Red produces good meat and brown-shelled eggs.

Polish has unusual feathers and is often in shows.

All About Chickens

Chickens have a lot in common with other birds. They have feathers, wings, and a beak. But some parts are unusual. Every chicken has a fleshy red comb on its head and pouch-like wattles under its beak. Chickens have large earlobes, too.

FUN FACT

Do you know these chicken names?
*A **pullet** is a young hen.*
*A **cockerel** is a young rooster.*

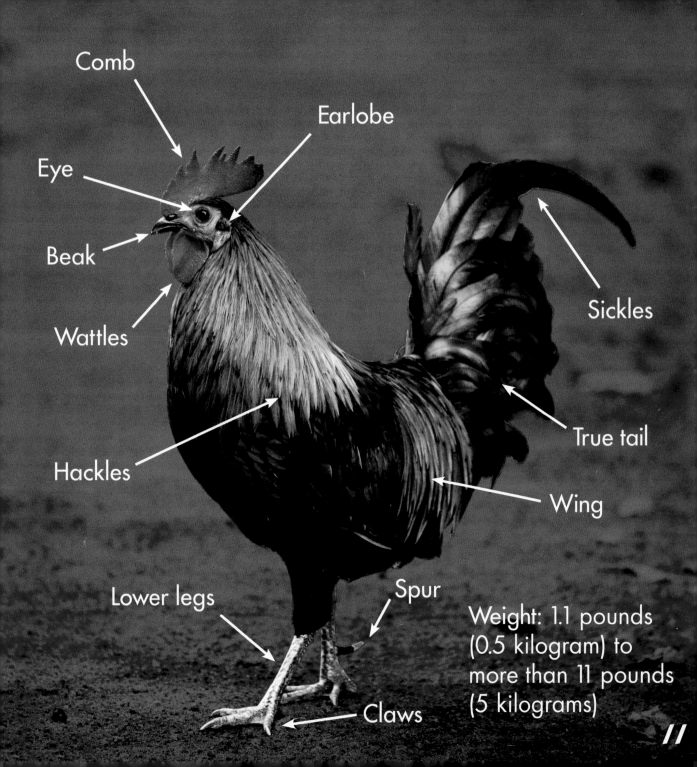

Comb

Earlobe

Eye

Beak

Wattles

Hackles

Sickles

True tail

Wing

Lower legs

Spur

Claws

Weight: 1.1 pounds (0.5 kilogram) to more than 11 pounds (5 kilograms)

Chickens have short wings that cannot easily lift up their big bodies. Because of this, chickens usually fly only when they need to flee from their enemies.

FUN FACT

Chickens have good eyesight during the day, but they see poorly at night.

13

Chickens find food by scratching and **pecking**. Using their claws, they scratch and dig into the soil to see what is there. They also use their beaks to peck at the ground in search of seeds and insects.

FUN FACT

Chickens have a special stomach called a gizzard. Its moving walls grind the chicken's food into tiny pieces. Bits of sand that the chicken swallowed earlier also help grind the food.

Farm Life

Chickens live on different types of farms. Some farms raise free-range chickens. On these farms, the **flock** of chickens spend the day in a pasture where there is plenty to eat. At night, these chickens sleep, or **roost**, inside a **coop**.

On some free-range chicken farms, each rooster helps protect a group of 12 to 20 hens.

On other chicken farms, chickens live in cages inside big buildings. The owners feed them a dry mix of foods and vitamins to keep them healthy. The chickens always have water to drink, too.

To save space, the farm owners often stack cages on top of each other.

More Chickens

Hens begin laying eggs at about 5 months old. Most hens lay one egg per day. To lay an egg, a hen does not need to mate with a rooster. When she does mate, her eggs will hatch into chicks.

FUN FACT
It takes 21 days for a chick to hatch from an egg.

People everywhere eat chicken eggs and meat to keep strong and healthy. For that reason, we owe the chickens of the world our thanks.

Glossary

breeds (breedz): different groups of animals; the animals in each group have a lot in common

cockerel (KOK-ur-ul): a rooster less than one year old

coop (KOOP): a small building or pen where chickens or others small animals stay

flock (FLOK): a group of animals that live, eat, or travel together

pecking (PEK-ing): striking or hitting many times with a beak

poultry (POHL-tree): farm birds raised for their meat and eggs

pullet (PUL-ut): a hen less than one year old

quality (KWAHL-uh-tee): important feature or part of someone or something

roost (ROOST): to rest or sleep on; birds often roost high above the ground on a branch or other place, called a perch

Index

Websites to Visit

www.flyingskunk.com/

www.kidsfarm.com/

www.lifelab.org/webcam.php

www.feathersite.com/Poultry/BRKChickensA-C.html

About the Author

Susan Markowitz Meredith enjoys learning new things about animals, including those on the farm. She especially likes to share what she discovers with young readers. Many of her 50+ books have been about animals, nature, and the way things work. Ms. Meredith has also produced quite a few TV shows for young thinkers.